Growing Up

Adria F. Klein

DOMINIE PRESS

Pearson Learning Group

Publisher: Christine Yuen
Series Editors: Adria F. Klein & Alan Trussell-Cullen
Editors: Bob Rowland & Paige Sanderson
Designers: Gary Hamada & Lois Stanfield
Photographers: Aaron Schall (pages 4, 5); SuperStock (Page 6 – kitten); Rose Waldie (Page 7 – cat); SuperStock (Page 8 – caterpillar, Page 9 – butterfly); K. Adria (Page 10 – baby).

Copyright ©2001 Dominie Press, Inc. All rights reserved. No part of this publication may be reproduced or transmitted in any form or by any means without permission in writing from the publisher. Reproduction of any part of this book, through photocopy, recording, or any electronic or mechanical retrieval system, without the written permission of the publisher, is an infringement of the copyright law.

Published by:

Dominie Press, Inc.

1949 Kellogg Avenue
Carlsbad, California 92008 USA

www.dominie.com

ISBN 0-7685-1510-6

Printed in Singapore by PH Productions Pte Ltd

7 8 9 10 11 10 09 08

Table of Contents

I see a puppy.

When it grows up, it will be a dog.

I see a kitten.

When it grows up, it will be a cat.

I see a caterpillar.

When it grows, it will be a butterfly.

When I grow,
I will be a big boy.

Picture Glossary

boy:

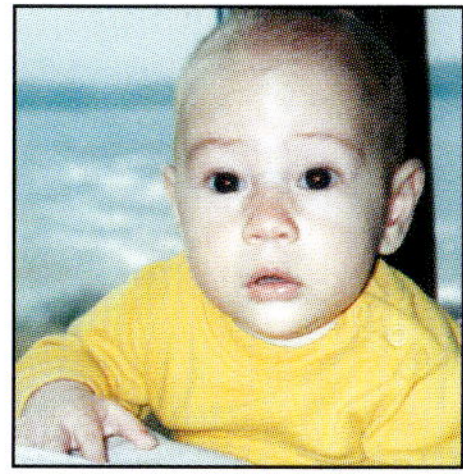

kitten:

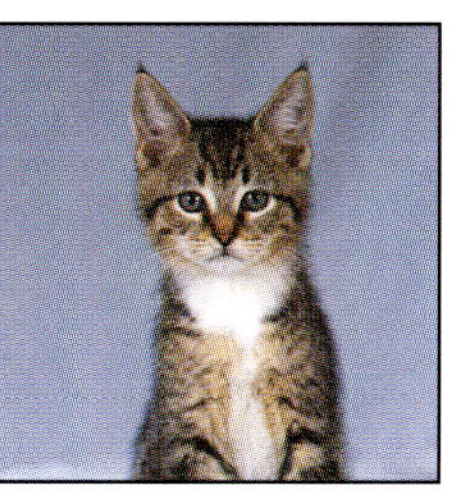

butterfly:

puppy:

Index